SIX PIECES

FOR SOLO PIANO

by

OTTORINO RESPIGHI

CONTENTS

Alla Signora Cesarina Donini Crema.

Valse Caressante.

Tempo lento di Valzer.

O. RESPIGHI.

PIANO.

MASTERS MUSIC PUBLICATIONS, INC.

4

CANONE

OTTORINO RESPIGHI

Andantino

Tempo Iº

NOTTURNO.

OTTORINO RESPIGHI

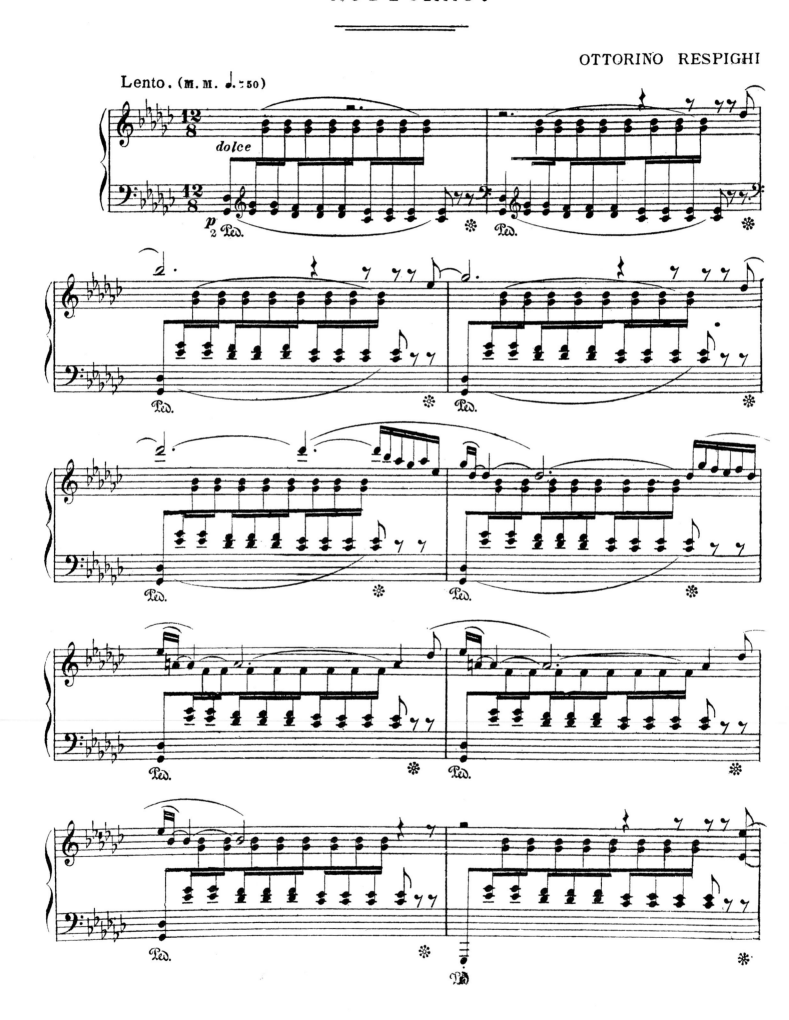

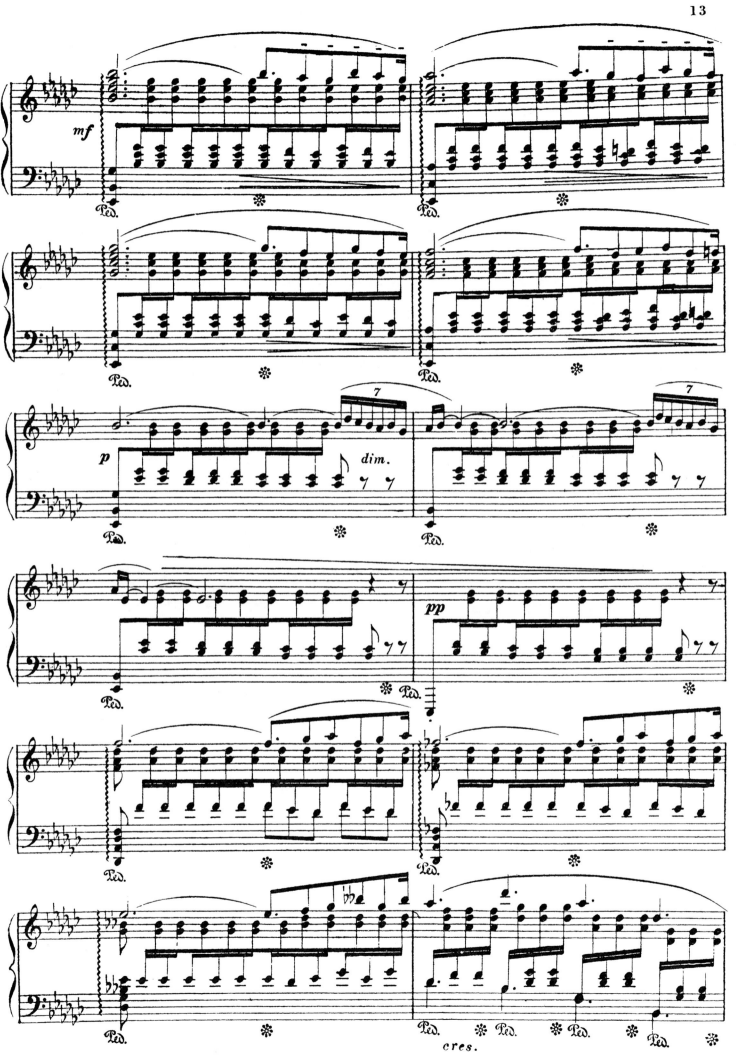

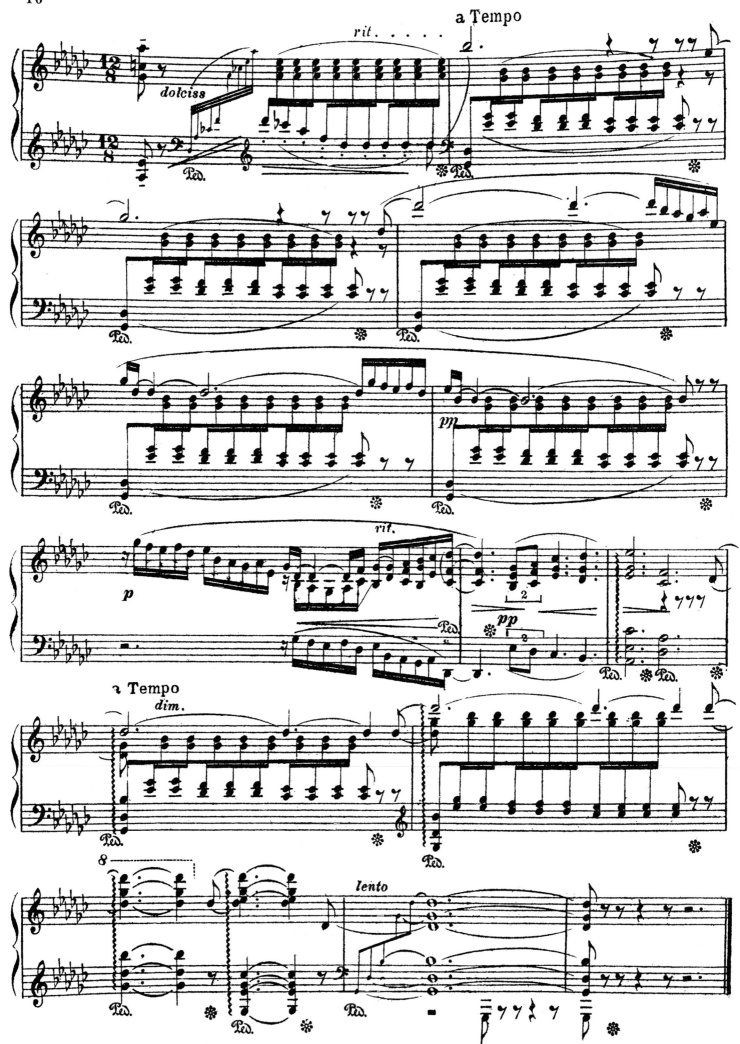

Alla Signorina ADELE RIGHI

MINUETTO

N.º 3.

OTTORINO RESPIGHI

ALLA CONTESSA IDA PERACCA CANTELLI

STUDIO

OTTORINO RESPIGHI

INTERMEZZO-SERENATA

(nell'opera comica Re Enzo)

O. RESPIGHI

Andante calmo

Selected Piano Publications

SOLO, UNACCOMPANIED

BIZET, GEORGES

M161091   Chants Du Rhin

The Chants du Rhin (Songs of the Rhine) is a cycle of six dreamy miniatures based on poems by Joseph Méry and composed in 1865. The songs are grouped symmetrically around the central "La bohémienne," revealing the beautiful and free-spirited gypsy girl as the overall theme. Bizet would return to the gypsy theme one year later in La jolie fille de Perth, and most famously ten years later in the opera, Carmen.

CHAMINADE, CECILE

W100391   Childrens Piano Album Bk. 1

The first "Children's Piano Album" (Op. 123) was written in 1906, with the second series (Op. 126) written the year after. Each contains 12 harmonically interesting pieces written for children. Book 1 includes the following pieces: 1. Prelude 2. Intermezzo 3. Canonetta 4. Rondeau 5. Gavotte 6. Gigue 7. Romance 8. Barcarolle 9. Orientale 10. Tarentelle 11. Air de Ballet 12. Marche Russe

W100491   Childrens Piano Album, Bk. 2 (Op. 126)

The first "Children's Piano Album" (Op. 123) was written in 1906, with the second series (Op. 126) written the year after. Each contains 12 harmonically interesting pieces written for children. Book 2 includes the following songs: 1. Idylle, 2. Aubade, 3. Rigaudon, 4. Eglogue, 5. Ballade, 6. Scherzo Valse, 7. Élégie, 8. Novelette, 9. Patrouille, 10. Villanelle, 11. Conte de Fées, 12. Valse Mignonne.

M260491   Etudes de Concert, Op. 35

A reprint edition of this important piano work by the turn-of-the-century French composer, Cécile Chaminade (1857-1944). Affiliating herself with nationalist composers such as Saint-Saëns and Gounod, her style was very much rooted in both Romantic and French tradition, her tuneful and highly accessible works were also tremendous favorites in the United States. These six Études de concert, Op. 35, date from around 1885, as Chaminade was moving away from the salon-style pieces where she started to the successful concert tours on which she had begun to embark, and which would give her international fame. That said, while the Études de concert are larger works compared to her earlier salon pieces, they are not overly bombastic or virtuosic. Movements: 1. Scherzo, 2. Automne, 3. Fileuse, 4. Appassionato, 5. Impromptu, 6. Tarantelle.

M276191   Theme Varie, Op. 89

COLERIDGE-TAYLOR, SAMUEL

M304191   24 Negro Melodies, Op. 59, Bk. 1

The transcription of melodies contained in this collection has been praised as "the most complete expression of Mr. Coleridge-Taylor's native bent and power." Using native songs of Africa and the West Indies with those that came into being in America during slavery, he has preserved their distinctive characteristics and individuality, while giving them an art form fully infused with their musical essence.

COWELL, HENRY

M329191   Three Irish Legends

Henry Dixon Cowell was an American composer, music theorist, pianist, teacher, publisher, and impresario. In the early 1950's, his music was summed up by Virgil Thomson as having "a wider range in both expression and technique than that of any other living composer...No other composer of our time has produced a body of works so radical and so normal, so penetrating and so comprehensive."

Cowell's Three Irish Legends remains one of the composer's most performed and recognizable compositions, and is noted for its striking use of tone clusters. The work is comprised of three movements: 1. The Tides of Manaunaun, 2. The Hero Sun, and 3. The Voice of Lir.

DETT, ROBERT NATHANIEL

M321691   In The Bottoms

"In the Bottoms" is a Suite of five numbers giving pictures of moods or scenes peculiar to African-American life in the river bottoms of the South. It is similar in its expression, and in a way continuation, of the sentiments already set forth in the "Magnolia Suite," but suggests ideas incidental to life in a more particular geographic territory. Movements: 1. Prelude (Night) 2. His Song 3. Honey (Humoresque) 4. Barcarolle (Morning) 5. Dance (Juba)

M398291   Magnolia Suite

Robert Nathaniel Dett was a Canadian-American Black composer, organist, pianist, choral director, and music professor. Born and raised in Canada until the age of 11, he moved to the United States with his family and had most of his professional education and career there. The Magnolia Suite for solo piano is in five movements: 1. Magnolias (D Major), 2. The Deserted Cabin (B minor), 3. My Lady Love (A Major), 4. Mammy (D flat Major), The Place Where the Rainbow Ends (G flat Major).

GERSHWIN, GEORGE

M388291   Novelette In Fourths

Transcribed and edited by Richard Dowling. First Edition. As played by George Gershwin on Welte-Mignon Piano Roll #3968, mid-1919. Includes biographical information about the composer and his relationship to the player piano.

GLIERE, REINHOLD

M331691   12 Children's Pieces

12 Children's Pieces (12 Pièces Enfantines, Op.31) by Reinhold Gliere is a collection of medium-difficulty pieces written for young pianists. Contents: Prélude; Nocturne; Berceuse; Rêverie; Chanson populaire; Valse; Romance; Etude; Mazurka; Chant oriental; Feuillet d'album; Air de Ballet.

MACDOWELL, EDWARD

M178991   Six Poems after Heinrich Heine, Op. 31

A set of little-known piano pieces by Edward MacDowell. Each work is preceded by a corresponding Heinrich Heine poem. Reprint of the first edition.

MARTINU, BOHUSLAV

Solc, Karel

M108591   Puppets, Book 1

Czech composer Bohuslav Martinu's first successful publication, "Puppets" is a cycle of 14 short pieces over a series of three books inspired by famous Italian puppets Pierrot, Columbine, and Harlequin. All three books are available from the publisher.

PROKOFIEV, SERGEI

W730791   10 Pieces, Op. 12

This collection of 10 short pieces by Sergei Prokofiev ranges in style and difficulty and can be performed in its entirety or individually.

M257891   Four Pieces, Op. 4

Composed with the intent to make a name for himself as both a composer and pianist, it is no surprise that Prokofiev's first four opuses are impressive, technical piano works. Movement Titles: I. Remembrance II. Soaring III. In despair IV. Devilish inspiration.

M273691   Visions fugitives, Op. 22

"Visions fugitives" is a cycle of 20 piano miniatures written between 1915 and 1917, many for friends of the composer. The miniatures are vignette-like, and the overall effect is Impressionist in style.

RAVEL, MAURICE

M225791   Le Tombeau de Couperin

The word "tombeau" is a musical term from the 17th century, meaning "a piece written as a memorial." Maurice Ravel (1875-1937) composed LE TOMBEAU DE COUPERIN as a six-movement suite (based on those of the Traditional Baroque suite) for solo piano, with each movement dedicated to the memory of a friend who had died fighting in World War I. The "Couperin" referred to in the title is François Couperin "the Great" (1668-1733), although Ravel's intentions were to pay homage to the sensibilities of the Baroque French keyboard suite in general, not one composer in general. Often light-hearted rather than sombre as one may suggest, Ravel responded, "The dead are sad enough, in their eternal silence." Movements: I. Prelude, II. Fugue, III. Forlane, IV. Rigaudon, V. Menuet, VI. Toccata.

SAINT SAENS, CAMILLE

M268391   Six Etudes, Op. 111

Saint-Saens' Opus 111 was first published in 1899, and each of the six etudes are dedicated to a different piano virtuoso. Etudes: 1. Tierces majeures et mineures 2. Traits chromatiques 3. Prelude et Fugue 4. Les Cloches de Las Palmas 5. Tierces majeures chromatiques 6. Toccata

M231291   Six Etudes, Op. 135

Saint-Saens' Op. 135 is a unique set of six neo-classical etudes written for the left hand only. Ravel studied these etudes when writing his "Concerto for the Left Hand." Etudes: 1. Prelude 2. Alla fuga 3. Moto perpetuo 4. Bourree 5. Elegie 6. Gigue

SATIE, ERIK

M130491   Je te veux Waltz

"Je te veux" (I Want You) is a waltz composed by Satie and dedicated to vocalist Paulette Darty. The song, utilizing erotic text by Henry Pacory, was first performed at La Scala cabaret in Paris. Versions for Vocal/Piano and Solo Piano are available from the publisher.

KEISERSOUTHERNMUSIC.COM

Questions/ comments? info@laurenkeisermusic.com